SAUROPODS
(giant dinosaurs)
STEGOSAURS
(plated dinosaurs)
STEGOSAURS
(plated dinosaurs)
SAUROPODS
(giant dinosaurs)
ORNITHOPODS
(duck-billed dinosaurs)
SAUROPODS
(giant dinosaurs)

Contents

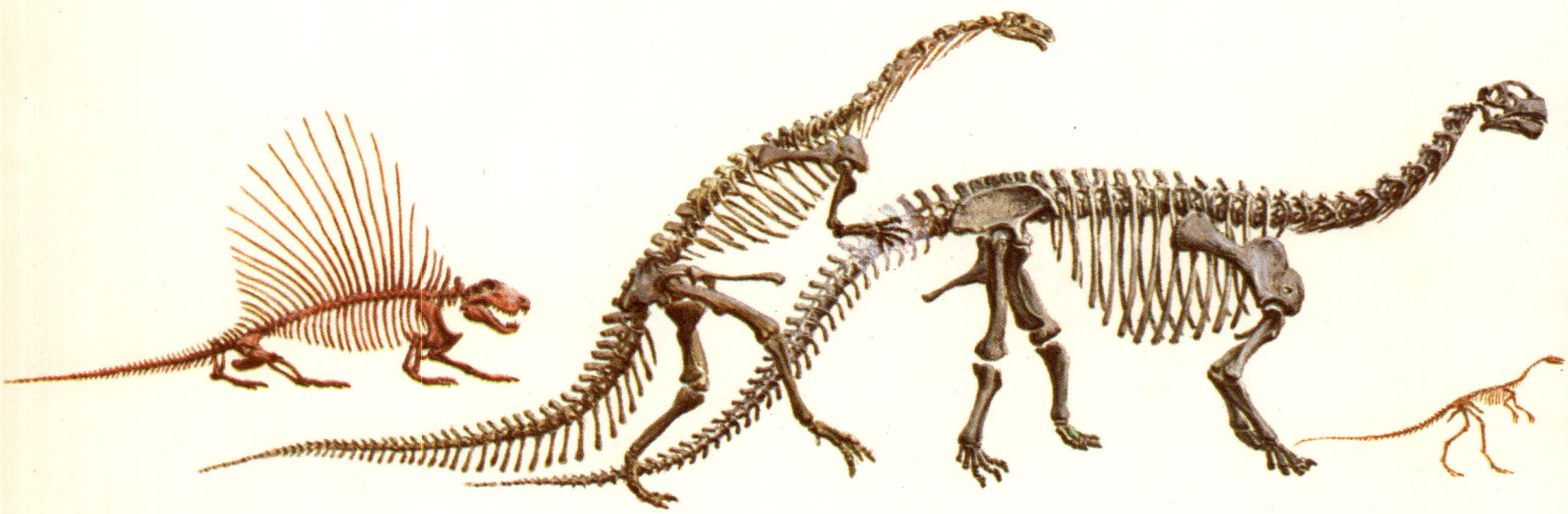

First Published 1966, Fifth Impression 1972
Published by The Hamlyn Publishing Group Limited
London • New York • Sydney • Toronto
Hamlyn House, Feltham, Middlesex, England

Printed in Czechoslovakia by VST Košice
ISBN 0 601 07175 1
51012
London · New York · Sydney · Toronto

U. K. Price 75p

Dinosaurs

and other Prehistoric Reptiles

by Jane Werner Watson

Illustrated by Rudolph F. Zallinger

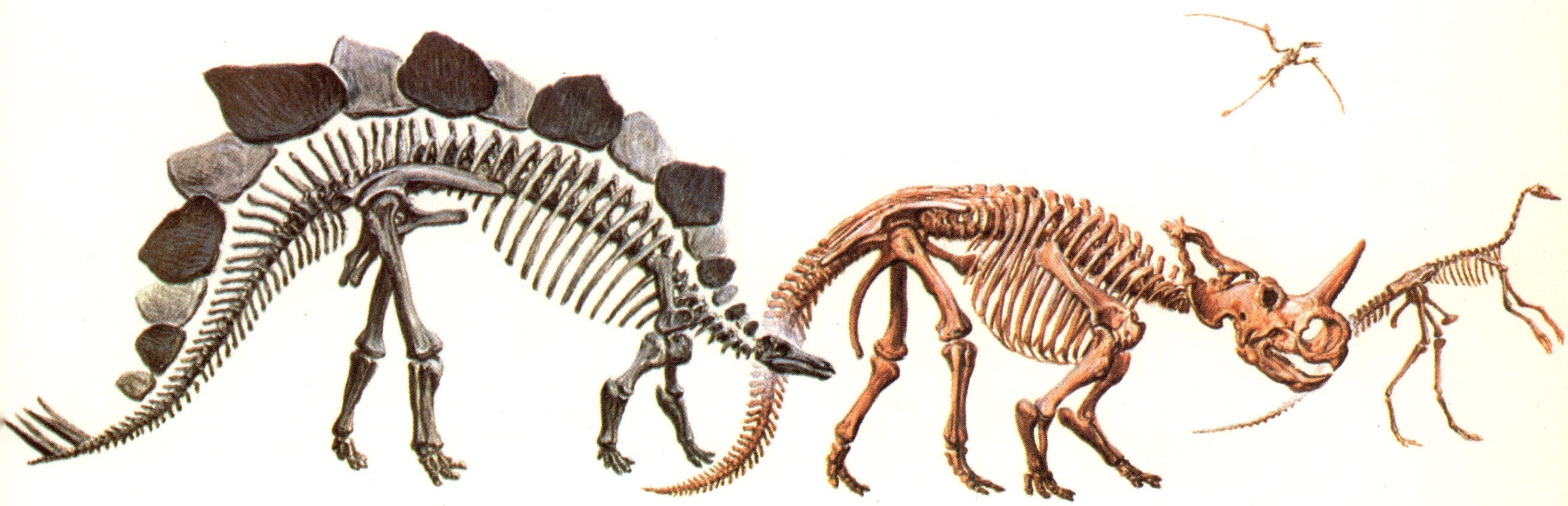

Hamlyn

London · New York · Sydney · Toronto

Fishes of the Devonian Period

Lobe-finned fishes of Devonian Period come on land.

BEFORE THE DINOSAURS

THE DINOSAURS LIVED long long ago. More than two hundred million years ago, the first dinosaurs appeared. About seventy million years ago, the last of them disappeared.

That is a long long time ago. It is hard for us to imagine such a long time, but let us try.

Perhaps the line at the bottom of the pages of this book will help us. It is a time line. It runs all the way back to the time of the first dinosaurs. The line below starts on the opposite page with the present, today. Each block or section stands for one million years.

Before man learnt to write his story he had lived for about half a million years. Man had spent a long time learning to gather food and to build shelters. He had spent a long time learning to live together in groups for safety against wild animals. All that time fits into the section between Historic Time, with the picture of the man hunting the woolly mammoth, and one million years.

Let us look back before the days of human beings. For long ages before man appeared, the chief kind of animals were mammals. Mammals are the furry kinds of animals we know best today,—the dogs and cats, the elephants and bears, wild beasts great and small. In those early times most mammals were tiny. Horses were only about the size of terriers today, for example.

What we call the Age of Mammals (or the Cenozoic Era) ends at one million years on our time line and had its beginning 70 million years ago, on page 15. At the same time that the Age of Mammals began, the Time of the Dinosaurs (or the Mesozoic Era) ended.

Turn to page 15 and you will see Struthiomimus, one of the last great dinosaurs to rule the earth before the days when mammals became common.

The Time of the Dinosaurs stretches back for page after page, through millions and millions of years, to two hundred million years ago. On page 32 of our time line the Mesozoic Era began, and the first dinosaurs appeared. But still the line goes on.

For the dinosaurs did not come out of nowhere. They developed from earlier and simpler animals. The time of these early animals (the Paleozoic Era) goes back from the Dimetrodon on page 32 to the end of the book and even further, far far beyond that, for we would need many more pages to carry the time line back to the beginning of that age. For that age began when the first animals came out of the sea and started living on shore.

The story of the dinosaurs really begins then.

HOW THE DINOSAURS CAME TO BE

This is the kind of fish that moved ashore to live on land. Its name is OSTEOLEPIS.

This is what early amphibians looked like when they had changed their fins to weak legs and feet. Its name is DIPLOVERTEBRON.

This is an amphibian after some ages of life on land. His name is ERYOPS. *He has grown larger. He can move about slowly on clumsy legs and is rather fierce. His kind still lays eggs in water.*

300 to 250 Million Years Ago

THREE hundred million years ago, all of earth's creatures lived in the seas. But very, very gradually some of them learned to live on land. In some places the fish swam up rivers and bays and learned to live in fresh water. Finally, there were fishes in rivers, lakes and ponds.

We do not know just what happened. Perhaps some fishes found themselves in rivers or ponds which dried up during certain seasons of the year. When they tried to swim, they flopped onto the mud.

Some of these ancient fishes were lung fishes. They could breathe air. (There are still lung fishes today which live in Africa, Australia and South America. When their rivers and lakes dry up during hot weather, they can still keep alive because they can breathe air.)

Among these ancient lung fishes were some with very strong fins. In water the fishes could move

This is an early reptile which could lay its eggs on land. It could live all its life on land. Its name is SEYMOURIA.

easily. They simply swayed along. Their tails pushed against the water. They steered with their two pairs of fins, and the water itself held them up.

On land it was harder to move but the lobe-finned lung fishes could drag themselves along with their fins.

Year after year after year, these fishes used their rounded fins like feet. They dragged themselves over the mud with their fins, to the next pond. Slowly, slowly those fins grew and changed. They grew longer and stronger. They were no longer needed for swimming. So they developed into what those creatures did need to live on land. Fins developed into legs and feet.

When plants or animals change or develop to fit the way they live, we call the change evolution.

These animals with lungs and feet were not fish any more. But they were not entirely land animals either. They still laid their eggs in water, and their babies lived in water until they grew up.

THIS KIND of creature we call an amphibian, which means "double life." There are still some amphibians which live today. Toads and frogs are amphibians. They live on land, but they lay their jelly-like eggs in water. There the eggs hatch into tadpoles, and the young tadpoles grow up in ponds.

This is an early reptile called a cotylosaur. His name is LIMNOSCELIS. *He has been extinct for 200 million years, but he was the ancestor of later reptiles.*

This is a tuatara (SPHENODON). *It is a little-changed survivor of the ancestors of lizards and dinosaurs. It is found in only one place in the world—on small islands in New Zealand.*

Well, ages went by. Amphibians developed stronger legs and backbones. They could walk without dragging themselves along the ground. They got along very well as long as there were plenty of swamps and ponds.

But the earth was changing. Many lands were being pushed up high above the seas. Many swamps and ponds dried up. This was hard on the amphibians, since they need water to lay their eggs in.

It was about this time that some amphibians made a great change. They began to lay eggs in hard shells.

These hard egg-shells protected the jelly-like eggs. Inside the shells were water and food for the tiny babies. So these eggs did not have to be laid in ponds. They could be laid on dry ground. And when the young animals came out of the eggs, they did not have to live in the water. They could live on land.

Now these animals no longer had to stay near the water. They could go where they pleased. They did not need water to lay their eggs in. They could live all their lives on land. They were a new kind of animal. We call them reptiles.

There are still some reptiles today. Lizards and snakes, turtles and crocodiles are reptiles. Crocodiles and turtles are usually found near the water. But some lizards and snakes live where it is very dry.

When reptiles had developed eggs that could be laid on land, they could live in many places where amphibians could not live. They found many new kinds of food.

DIMETRODON

EDAPHOSAURUS

Some ate fish. Some ate meat. Some ate plants, and they gradually developed different shapes of bones and teeth, to suit the ways they lived and ate. They developed into creatures of all sizes and of many habits.

Think of food. There have always been animals, on land or in the sea, which ate meat. We call them carnivores, meat-eaters. They are usually rather fierce, for they are hunters. They must kill to live.

Carnivores need long, sharp teeth for snatching and tearing food. They need swift legs for running after it.

There have always been plant-eaters too. We call them herbivores. Plant-eaters are usually meek and mild. Even a small carnivore is often fiercer than a big herbivore.

Plants do not run away. So plant-eaters do not need to be able to move fast to get food. (Though it is helpful to be able to run away from carnivores!) What plant-eaters need most is broad, blunt teeth. These are good for chopping up plant food. And they need large stomachs to digest food slowly.

Some reptiles developed teeth which fitted into deep cups in their jawbones. We call these cups "sockets." This whole group of reptiles, which lived about 200 million years ago, scientists call thecodonts. This name means "teeth-in-sockets."

GORGOSAURUS

Reptile-hip

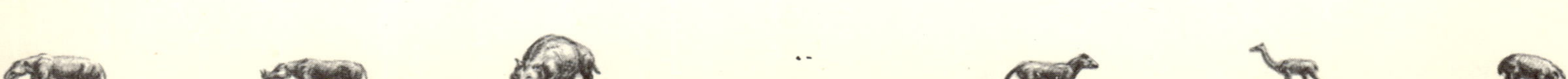

These "teeth-in-sockets" or thecodonts were mostly small animals, with light bones. Their new teeth were sharp. Their hind legs were strong, and they could raise the front part of their bodies from the ground. They could run swiftly. So they got plenty of food. They were successful animals. As ages passed, some of these "teeth-in-sockets" developed into dinosaurs.

WHAT is a dinosaur? When scientists began to find the bones of these animals of the past in rocks, they were impressed by their great size. The bones were much like those of some lizards of today. But they were much, much larger. So "terrible lizards" seemed a good name for these unknown animals. The word dinosaur comes from two Greek words, *deinos* and *sauros*. "Terrible Lizard" is what these words mean.

The dinosaurs were not lizards. Not all were terrifying. Many were not even very large. They did not even all belong to the same order of reptiles.

This is how the two orders of dinosaurs came to be. The split started with those swift, light-boned "teeth-in-socket" reptiles. As they raced about the woodlands after food, they found they could run faster on two legs than on four.

They began to run on their hind legs. They used their front legs for snatching at food. Gradually, through many thousands of years, these front limbs became shorter. Often they had hook-like claws on their feet. They developed long tails for balance.

To run on their hind legs, the animals had to hold their legs under their bodies, as birds do today, instead of sprawled out to the side, like lizards' legs. This change in leg position caused changes in the muscles of legs and hips and in the hip bones too.

Through ages of walking on hind legs, some of these animals developed "bird-hips." Bird-hips have especially deep sockets for the upper leg bones to fit into, and the backbone is especially strongly attached to the hip bones.

The bird-hips are one great order of dinosaurs. Scientists call them Ornithischia. Others made the change in hip bones in a different way. They make up the other great order of dinosaurs, and scientists call them Saurischia or "reptile-hips."

Later on some members of both groups went back to walking on all fours. But they retained the bird-like or reptile-like hip structure.

So to this day a scientist will look at the hip bones of a dinosaur and classify it as a bird-hip or a reptile-hip.

Dinosaurs are divided into two orders—the Saurischia or "reptile-hips" and the Ornithischia or "bird-hips."

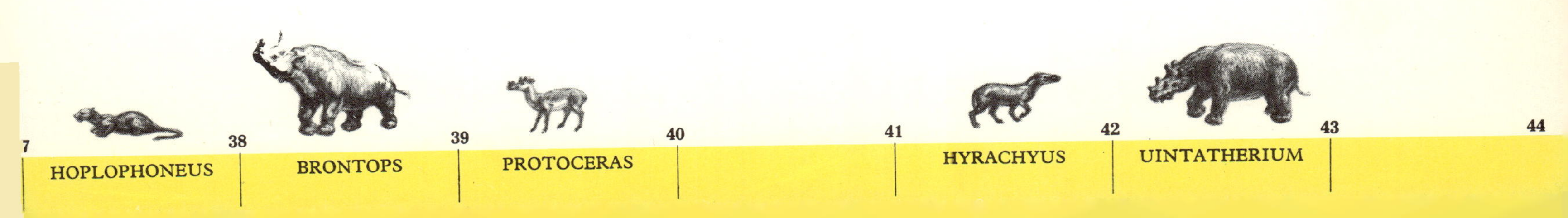

Fossils of plants and insect of the Carboniferous Period

THE SWAMPY WOODLAND

250 Million Years Ago in the Carboniferous Period

Let us take a look at the world of 250 million years ago.

Not a house, not a road, not a person do we see. There are no human beings on earth.

All around is swampy woodland. The ground is covered with small green plants. Underneath, it is squishy and damp.

Above, tower green tree-like plants. Some are giant ferns. Some look rather like palms. But these are not the trees we know today.

The air is warm and damp and still. And the world seems strangely silent. We do not hear the chirp or twitter of a single bird. We do not see the flutter of a feathered wing. There are no birds in the world.

In all the moist greenery we do not see a single flower. These plants do not have blossoms to produce their seeds. There are no flowers in this world.

We do not see many small, busy animals hurrying about. The small animals we know are mostly mammals. They had not yet appeared in this world of 250 million years ago.

Look! There is something moving. It looks like a bird, a big one, too. As we look more closely, we see that it has wings more than two feet across. But they are not feathered. They shimmer like glass. It is no bird but a giant dragonfly that we see.

There are many insects in the world, some of the same kinds we know today. We see a cobweb in the sunlight, hung with heavy drops of dew. So there are spiders, and scuttling underfoot are scorpions, cockroaches and many-footed millipedes.

Swampy woodland of the Carboniferous Period

SALTOPOSUCHUS PHYTOSAUR PROCOMPSOGNATHUS

THE FIRST OF THE DINOSAURS

180 Million Years Ago in the Triassic Period

SH! We hear a rustling in the greenery and a soft sound of running feet. A swift, small figure crosses the clearing.

We have a view of long legs on a small, smooth body, we see a long, thin tail whipping out behind. A pointed head on a long, thin neck turns this way and that, hunting for big juicy beetles.

This is Procompsognathus, an early meat-eating dinosaur. But how small it is! Procompsognathus is not much bigger than a good-sized turkey would be, stripped of its feathers and given a long, thin tail.

This is not our idea of a dinosaur. We expect them to be huge and powerful. But it took many millions of years for the dinosaurs to develop giants among them. Many of the early ones were quite small.

Sunning himself nearby is a Phytosaur. He looks like a crocodile. But he is a thecodont reptile. By the end of the Triassic Period his kind had disappeared.

There is another reptile now, the one with dark stripes like the rungs on a ladder down its back. Saltoposuchus is its name.

PLATEOSAURUS

It stands, when on its hind feet, about three feet tall. But it is really longer than that, from nose-tip to tail. For it does not stand up straight, as we do. It leans forward as it runs.

Saltoposuchus is a good example of the pre-dinosaur "teeth-in-sockets." It can run fast on its light, bird-like feet. It looks rather like a large lizard. Saltoposuchus is small enough to hide from bigger hunters. It has big eyes for finding smaller animals. It can catch them in sharp claws and tear them with sharp teeth set in strong jaws. Saltoposuchus is well built to take care of itself.

Procompsognathus is a meat-eater too. And he has found a meal. As he bends down, reaching with tiny forearms, we see what the meal is. It is a nest of big, pale-coloured eggs.

What animals can lay such big eggs? We wonder. We learn the answer soon enough. For here comes the mother. She does not usually look after her eggs, once they are laid. But she is not pleased to see this small hunter digging them out of their warm, moist nest of grasses. She stamps and threshes her long tail, and Procompsognathus runs.

The giant mother is Plateosaurus, Flat Lizard. She does not look flat to us! She must be twenty feet long from nose to tail. Her small head waves high on top of her long neck, and her eyes look wild.

Plateosaurus was the giant of the early days of dinosaurs. Like Saltoposuchus and Procompsognathus, she was reptile-hipped. She ran on her hind legs, but when she fed on green plants, she rested on her strong fore-limbs as well.

She was mainly a plant-eater, but her small relatives took no chances. They hid from her sight.

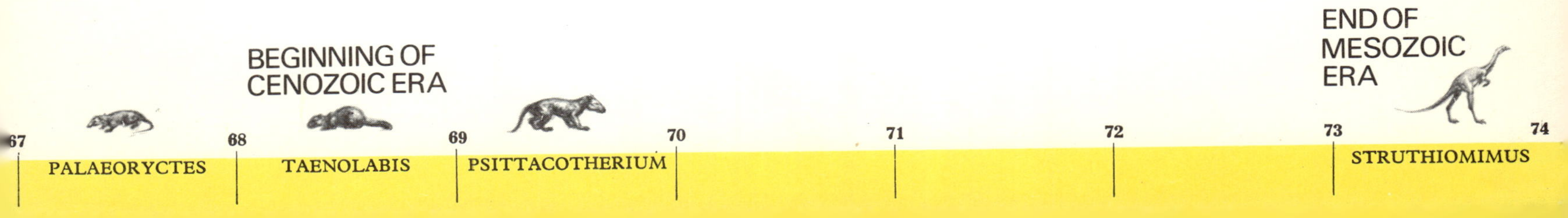

ORNITHOLESTES

ARCHAEOPTERYX

75 TRICERATOPS 76 million years ago 77

78 STYRACOSAURUS 79

80 MONOCLONIUS 81

Fossil remains of Archeopteryx

THE WARM, WIDE SEAS

150 Million Years Ago in the Jurassic Period

ALL AROUND we hear the soft slosh of water against the shores. The waters of the earth have risen. Shallow lakes and seas now cover much of what we know today as Europe and North America.

The sunshine beats down. Mist hangs over the water. The climate is warm and sticky. But plant life is doing very well. All around tower palms and huge, fern-like trees. Under them grows a tangle of green.

This is a time when plants which are found only in the tropics today grew almost to the North Pole. All over the earth, the climate is mild.

In the treetops we see the movement of a bird's wing. Surely it is a bird! It does not soar through the air. Instead, it seems to pull itself along in the trees, with the help of claws on its wings. Now and then it glides across an open space.

This is "Ancient Wing" or Archaeopteryx, the first true bird. It is about the size of the pigeons we see today.

Archaeopteryx still has some scales on its legs. For, like all birds, it developed from a reptile, and most of the scales have been replaced by light feathers. It still has a long, reptile tail, but the tail has feathers which help the bird to glide.

Not far away in the woods another small form flaps from tree to tree. This is "Ancient Bird" or Archaeornis. It is very, very similar to Archaeopteryx. Perhaps it is, in fact, the same.

These birds are light and swift-moving. They need to be. For there are many hungry hunters in the woods.

Here comes a swift dinosaur on the hunt. It is called Bird Stealer, Ornitholestes. Bird Stealer is about five feet long with a light body and long legs. It can run lightly on its two pronged feet. It can move very swiftly in the shadows, and it has long clutching fingers on its short forelegs. They are strong enough to snatch a bird from its perch. That is why men have given it this name.

OUT OVER the water, safe from Bird Stealer's reach, flies another creature. This is Prow Beak or Rhamphorhynchus. Prow Beak is not really a bird but a flying reptile. Instead of feathers it has a leathery skin.

Prow Beak's body is very small and light. Its bones are hollow. It has a long, sharp-beaked head and a long tail, but most important are its hands. One bony finger of each hand has grown very, very long. It supports a sheet of skin attached the whole length of the lizard's body. When Prow Beak raises his arms, these two sheets of skin become a pair of wings for gliding. He can really fly too. So his heart probably pumps warm blood through his body, though most reptiles are cold-blooded.

Prow Beak even has a sort of rudder on the end of his tail to help him steer. See! He glides down to the water, steering with the disk on the end of his tail. His large teeth grip a slippery fish, and away he goes.

We would like to see how he perches when he comes to rest. For scientists do not know whether Rhamphorhynchus used his feet, as birds do today, or hung by the "hands" on his wings, but we will not find out this time. For he disappears from sight.

As Prow Beak flies away, a pointed nose pokes up from the sea. It looks like a huge fish with a mouthful of sharp teeth, but really it is a reptile. This is Fish Lizard, or Ichthyosaurus. He is a reptile that went back to the sea to live. His feet turned into firm flippers. His long, thin lizard tail fanned out like a fish tail. His body became streamlined like that of a fish.

But Fish Lizards are not really fish. They still breathe air with lungs and have no fish gills. And the female does not lay eggs as a female fish does.

Instead the mother ichthyosaur keeps her eggs inside her own body. She hatches them safely there. Her babies are born alive, and live in the sea all their lives. They thrive so well in the sea that some of them grow to be 40 feet long!

Another reptile which has gone back to the sea is the Geosaurus. This inappropriate name means Earth Lizard. These reptiles are also called marine crocodiles. They are related to the crocodiles we know. But their four short legs have turned into paddles. They paddle through the water, and they push themselves along with their tails, as fishes do. They live all their lives in water. They never go ashore any more, it seems, except to lay their eggs.

ICHTHYOSAURUS

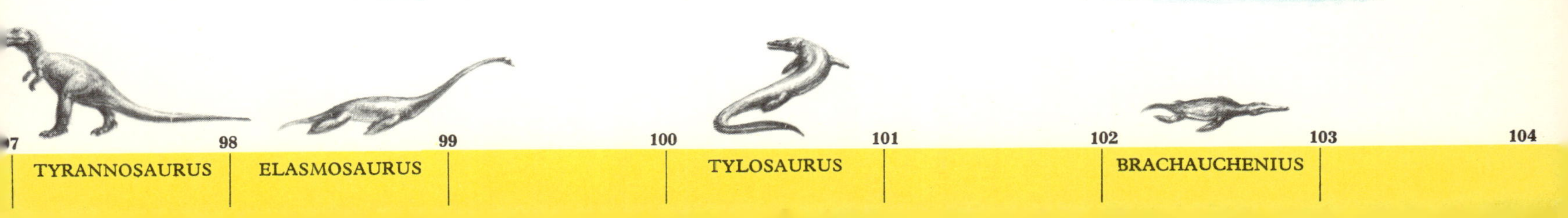

Far inland, up a river, where the water is fairly shallow, we see a strange sight. A pair of eyes and a pair of nostrils poke up above the still water. The bone around the nostrils forms a small dome. This dome belongs to Brachiosaurus, or Lizard Arm.

Lizard Arm is the heaviest of all dinosaurs. He weighs about fifty tons. As he thrusts his head up into the air, we see that he has a long, heavy neck. It is perched high on his heavy body. His huge front legs, or "arms," are longer and heavier than his back legs. They give him his name.

Brachiosaurus is so heavy that he needs four legs built like pillars to support his weight. But even they do not do it easily. This is one reason he stays in the water much of the time. The water helps to hold him up.

The other reason is safety. Brachiosaurus is very slow-moving and clumsy when he does have to lumber out onto land. He could never run from an enemy. He does not have much of a mind. His tiny brain weighs only a few ounces. It is not planned for quick reactions. So the safest thing to do is to hide.

Out in a quiet pool carpeted with water weeds, Brachiosaurus can eat and rest in peace. His neck is long enough to reach down to the bottom for greens, and his eyes are so arranged that he can keep a watch on things without being seen.

BRACHIOSAURUS

CRETACEOUS PERIOD
12
113
114
115
116
117
118
119
CETIOSAURUS
IGUANODON
PROTOCERATOPS
PSITTACOSAURUS

120 million years ago | 121 | 122 | 123 | 124 | 125 | 12

ORNITHOLESTES

ALLOSAURUS

Near by feeds Diplodocus, whose name means the Double Beamed. He is the longest of all dinosaurs. He measures as much as $87\frac{1}{2}$ feet, but he is more lightly and slimly built than Brachiosaurus.

Ashore, he walks with his long neck stretching far out in front to balance the long tail behind.

Diplodocus does not waste much time walking, for his head and mouth are tiny. His body is huge. As he can take only very small bites with his weak teeth, it takes a lot to make a meal for him.

So Diplodocus has to spend most of his time steadily eating to keep himself well fed.

DIPLODOCUS

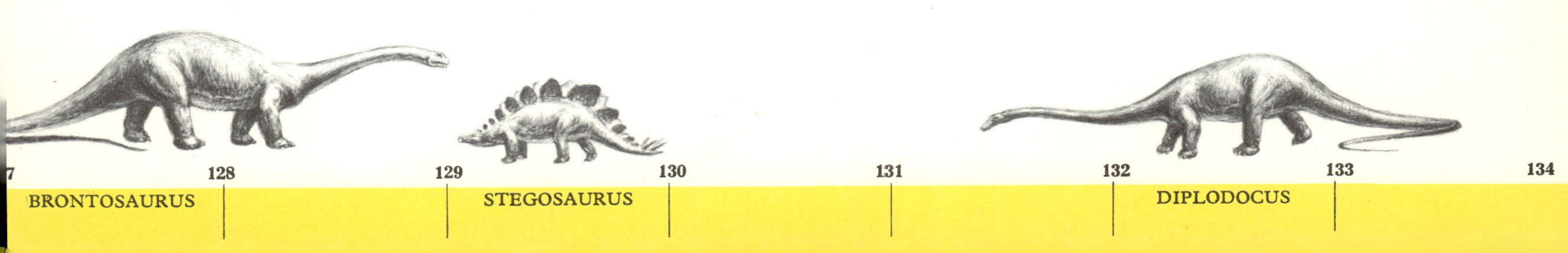

BRONTOSAURUS

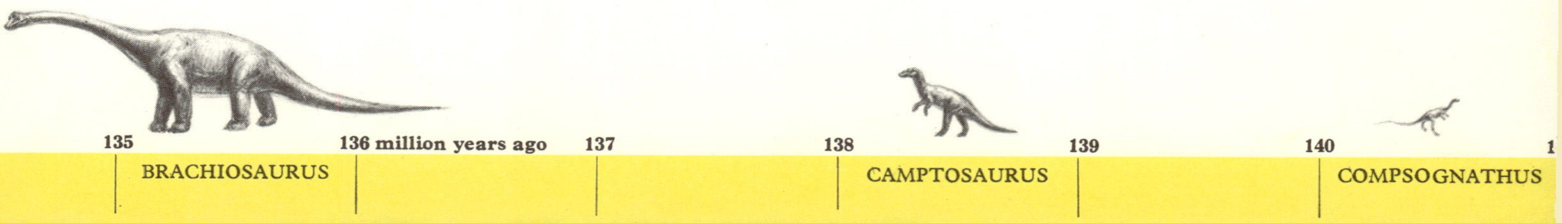

CAMPTOSAURUS

The third dinosaur giant is Brontosaurus, Thunder Lizard. Thunder Lizard does not go ashore much either. Like the two other giants, she is a peace-loving plant-eater. She is not as heavy as Brachiosaurus, nor as long as Diplodocus. But she does weigh thirty tons, and she is 67 feet long from nose to tail tip. So she too is most comfortable in the water, with the weight off her feet.

Today Brontosaurus has come ashore to lay some eggs. She has just finished smoothing sand and grasses over the nestful. Then she heads back for the safety of the water, but today is not her lucky day. Allosaurus the hunter has caught sight of her!

Allosaurus is not interested in eggs, and he does not care for plants to eat. He likes meat—great chunks of fresh meat! He is big—35 feet long.

Allosaurus has sharp claws at the ends of his short forelegs. They can get a grip and really hold on. His teeth are big and sharp, and he has a tremendous appetite.

Standing on his hind legs, Allosaurus balances himself by leaning on his muscular tail. He watches Brontosaurus lumbering along, heading for the safety of the water.

Allosaurus blows out his breath in a great snort and takes off after his prey. Just at the shore he leaps.

What a battle this is! Allosaurus sinks his sharp claws into Brontosaurus's meaty shoulder. But the plant-eater whips around her great tail and knocks the hunter back.

Brontosaurus plunges out into shallow water, and Allosaurus strikes again. His jaws close upon her neck. Brontosaurus cannot save herself now, but as she sinks, she throws her great weight upon the killer. Allosaurus, with his jaws still locked about Bronto's neck, is pushed beneath the water. Thirty tons pin him, helpless, in the sand.

Up the shore Camptosaurus, Bent Lizard, lifts his head from a meal of fresh-water plants. He rears up on his hind legs to watch.

Soon the water rolls peacefully over the hidden forms. Slowly a layer of shifting sand blankets killer and victim alike... And so the years pass by.

42 143 144 145 146 147 148 149

GEOSAURUS

150 PLESIOSAURUS 151 million years ago 152 153 ARCHEOPTERYX 154 155 15

ANKYLOSAURUS

THE FLOWERING LAND

120 Million Years Ago in the Cretaceous Period

WHAT a change has come upon the earth! The air feels fresher and cooler. It is not moist and sticky now. We are not surrounded by swamps and seas any more. Here we see a rolling country with woods of oak and hickory. Down in the hollows where the streams run, we see the pale green of willows, and through the shadowy woods we catch glimpses of flowers. For flowering plants have appeared!

Flowering plants are new in the world, and there is a new sound to go with them. It is a familiar sound to us. It is the buzzing of bees. Bees began their work of spreading flower pollen as far back as 120 million years ago. They are still busy at it today.

There are dinosaurs here too. But some of the old giants have died out. Brontosaurus, Diplodocus, Brachiosaurus, all have vanished. As the wide, shallow waters dwindled, perhaps there was not enough green plant food left to feed all these hungry giants. So through the ages fewer of them grew up. They laid fewer eggs. And at last there were none at all, except in what is now South America.

New groups of dinosaurs, whose bodies are protected, appear now. They cannot run rapidly for protection from hunters. So they have developed their own protection. These dinosaurs wear coats of armour.

An early armoured dinosaur which lived in the Jurassic Period was Stegosaurus, Plated Lizard. The tall, stiff armour plates standing up from his high-curved, 20-foot-long back looked hard to bite, and no one wanted that tail with its sharp two-foot spikes swung at him. So most enemies left Stegosaurus alone.

All the armoured dinosaurs were bird-hipped, including Stegosaurus. His hind legs were long and strong. His hip bones were firmly fitted to his backbone, and, though he walked on all fours, his front legs were short, as with most bird-hips.

New armoured dinosaurs are seen now. Ankylosaurus or Curved Lizard is one. His name comes from his curved ribs. He has a wide, flat body. His back is covered with thick plates of bone. His legs are short, and he is built low to the ground. As he

57 158 159 160 161 162 163 164

walks through the woods, he looks almost like a giant horned toad.

All around the edge of his armour coat he wears a set of long spikes. They stand out straight. They do not look tasty to a hunter. His long tail has a heavy knot on the end. He can swing this tail like a club. So most meat-eating dinosaurs leave him alone.

IGUANODON

HERE WE ARE back at a swampy shore. For there still are great swamps and lakes and seas in the world. Along the shores still live many dinosaurs. These are not the huge, reptile-hipped giants of old. These are a newer, bird-hipped family, the duck-bills.

The first of this sort, though not truly a duck-bill, was Camptosaurus or Bent Lizard. We saw him, you remember, back twenty million years or more. Then he was quietly munching water plants with his horny-beaked bill. He managed to stay out of reach of the giant hunters. For, being only five to eight feet tall, he was no match for the giants.

Now an age has passed. The giants of old have vanished. But a relative of Camptosaurus, Iguanodon, is still around, still munching away. His name means Iguana Tooth. He has grown much larger than Bent Lizard. This one must be thirty feet long. He has a thick, heavy tail and a spike for a thumb.

A later relative of Iguanodon is duck-billed Anatosaurus. He comes swimming easily into shore. His heavy tail sweeps the water behind him. His hind limbs are stronger and longer than the forelimbs and as he wallows ashore he rears up on his hind legs and leans back to balance his tail. Now we see that he, too, is much larger than Bent Lizard. He has webs between his digits which help him to move while he is looking for food.

Anatosaurus shakes the water from his leathery skin and opens wide his flat, broad, duck-bill jaws. With these jaws he probably can eat plants that grow under water, just as can the dabbling ducks we know today. Now we see why he was given his name. Look at those teeth! A thousand teeth pave his lower jaw like a rough cobblestone street. A thousand more in his upper jaw help grind his meals of water plants. He has more teeth than any other reptile.

Because he is such a large animal he needs a great deal of nourishment to sustain him and so he stays close to his food supplies nibbling steadily all day to maintain his strength and usually browsing contentedly. The only time he runs fast is when pursued by a ferocious meat-eating dinosaur.

JURASSIC PERIOD

165 million years ago 166 167 168 169 170 171

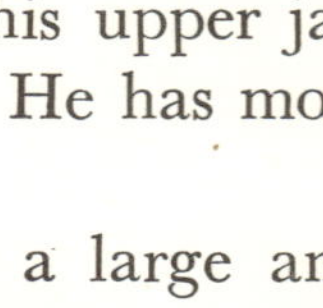

PLATEOSAURUS

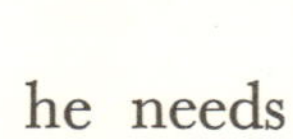

CYNOGNATHUS

ANATOSAURUS

All the duck-bills stay near the water. They waddle along the shores, now on two feet, again on four. Some of them prefer to be in the water, and some even like to stay under it!

How do they manage to stay under water? They really do not breathe there. They have special air storage spaces built into their skulls. These bones look like crested caps or helmets from the outside, but inside are hollow spaces to hold a small supply of air. This structure keeps water out of the windpipe while the animal feeds under water. Let's see how it works.

Two of these duck-bills are on the shore. One is Corythosaurus whose bony head looks as if he were wearing a helmet. The other is Parasaurolophus who has a bony crest on his head.

GORGOSAURUS

Here comes danger! The danger is Gorgosaurus, a giant hunter. He belongs to the family of old Allosaurus. But he is larger still, and he is hungry most of the time.

Corythosaurus, the Helmet Lizard, and Parasaurolophus, Like-a-Crested-Lizard, see their danger. They race for the water. Out they splash, deeper and deeper. As they swim on the surface they take deep breaths. They fill their hollow skulls with air, and down they go to the bottom. That is a good way to escape dangers on the shore, and it also gets them to more succulent plants.

CORYTHOSAURUS PARASAUROLOPHUS

180 million years ago 181 182 183 184 185 18

SALTOPOSUCHUS

PSITTACOSAURUS

FROM THE PLAINS OF MONGOLIA TO THE UPLANDS OF NORTH AMERICA

100 to 90 Million Years Ago

On the high open plains a new family has become large and successful. This family is the horned dinosaurs. They have come a long way since the day of their ancestor Psittacosaurus, seen above.

Psittacosaurus is a strange little fellow. He has a sharp, pointed beak, shaped something like a parrot's beak. So the scientists, who found his bones in the Gobi Desert, call him Parrot Lizard. He does not look like much of a dinosaur to us. But wait and see what his family develops into! For Parrot Lizard is the great grandfather of the horned dinosaurs, the last of the great dinosaur families.

On the next page we see one of the first of these horned dinosaurs. Men call him Protoceratops or First Horned Face. He lived on the dry plains of Mongolia. He is not very large, perhaps six or eight feet long. A family often starts out small and grows larger through the ages. That is what the horned dinosaurs did.

Protoceratops is quite fierce-looking, though. For behind his parrot beak he wears a wide, bony cap. It stands out fiercely around his face.

To be sure, Protoceratops does not have horns. But his parrot beak and the long frill of bones which goes from the back of his skull out over his neck show that he is an ancestor of all the horned dinosaurs that appeared later.

Protoceratops walks on all four of his legs. But his front legs are shorter than his hind legs. At some long distant time in the past, his forefathers may possibly have walked on only their hind legs.

Tasty meals of green plants are all the food that Protoceratops ever eats. Most of the time he can munch away without being disturbed. For the

PROTOCERATOPS

meat-eating dinosaurs of his day have learned that sturdy Protoceratops can put up a good fight if he has to, so they usually leave him alone.

Look at the ground here. A female Protoceratops has laid a nestful of eggs in a sandy hollow. The eggs look very large to us. Each egg is about eight inches long. The shell and the shape of the shell looks almost like turtle eggs we would find in our own time.

Watch! One egg, then another begins to quiver and crack. They are ready to hatch. The first baby crawls out. It has no bony cap as yet. That will come as it grows up. Now it is just very small and weak, and from the looks of things, it may not live to grow up. For here comes a hungry hunter.

The hunter is very small for a dinosaur, only about three feet long. Although he is hungry, meat is not the kind of meal he wants, for he has no

OVIRAPTOR

teeth. Sucking eggs is his idea of a feast. This is why scientists of today call him Oviraptor which means Egg Stealer. If he cannot find eggs, he will make do with fruits and other soft foods.

But today he has found a banquet, a whole nest of eggs. They are ready to hatch. Perhaps Oviraptor could manage to eat a soft-boned, newly hatched Protoceratops. We cannot be sure. Because he does not have time to eat this meal.

The sky darkens. A cold wind rises. The wind sends stones rattling across the ground. It sends clouds of sand rolling and tumbling. Oviraptor feels the sting of the needle-like sand grains. He crouches on the nest, hiding his head. The sand slithers along. It piles up, drifting over the nest and eggs. It drifts over Oviraptor too.

The wind dies down. The sand settles, and now the desert is bare of life.

GORGOSAURUS

STYRACOSAURUS

ACROSS THE OCEAN in a distant land which we now know as North America, we find more horned dinosaurs of a somewhat later time.

Here, coming upon them too, is Gorgosaurus. We know him as the Terrible Lizard. He can smell meat near by. So he is stamping about, looking for it.

First he comes face to face with Styracosaurus, or Spike Lizard, and what a face this is to meet! A long, sharp horn tilts upward from Spike Lizard's parrot-beaked nose. But that is not all. He wears a great frill of horn standing up on his head, and the frill is decked with sharp spikes all along its edge.

210 million years ago | 211 | 212 | 213 | 214 | 215 | 2

Gorgosaurus strides forward. Spike Lizard's watchful eyes follow every step. He moves his sharp horn slowly from side to side.

Before that threat Gorgosaurus weakens. His hide already bears the scars of that sharp horn. He wants no more of it. Snuffling with rage, he backs and turns away.

Next he meets Monoclonius, or Single Horn. Monoclonius is big enough to make a good meal. But there are other things to consider. The "single horn" for which this dinosaur is named is long and sharp. It grows from his nose.

As Monoclonius stands with his great head lowered, that sharp horn is tilted straight at Terrible Lizard. Above Monoclonius' eyes small horns glint in the sunlight. Gorgosaurus decides he is not hungry enough to tackle this horned giant either. He moves on, hungry still.

MONOCLONIUS

217 218 219 220 221 222 223 224

TRICERATOPS

VARANOPS

225 million years ago 226 227 228 229

SEYMOURIA

230 231

PTERANODON

THE LAST OF THE GIANTS

70 Million Years Ago

The earth has been changing again. Slowly, slowly, huge sections of land have been pushed up, up. Once, millions of years before, they had lain at the bottom of a shallow sea. Now they have been pushed far above the waters. The seas have shrunk back. Some of these lands are now high, dry plains.

In other places huge sheets of rock have been squeezed between other rocks. Through long ages they have been squeezed and squeezed. At the end of this era they will buckle and crack. They will crumple like a paper you crush in your hand. Instead of lying flat they will rise up into many high, sharp-peaked new mountains.

Far out at sea leathery-winged Pteranodon or Toothless Wing tilts his twenty-foot wings and glides with the wind. His big, sharp eyes scan the water below for food.

Pteranodon dips down and snatches a fish from the sea. On the ground he can move only awkwardly. His hind legs are small and weak, and he does not have much sense of smell.

Pteranodon is probably warm-blooded. Warm blood is a big advantage. His heart must pump very fast to keep him flying for long times as he hunts. Other reptiles are cold-blooded. They need sunlight and warmth to give them energy.

Back on land new warm-blooded animals are appearing. They are the furry mammals. They live mainly among the trees. For branches thick with leaves make good hiding places, and these small creatures must hide away to be safe.

A small mammal has come out hunting for insects and seeds. He wears a coat of fur, and his heart pumps warm blood through his body.

Near by is Giant Triceratops, Three-Horn-Face, one of the cold-blooded dinosaurs. He sniffs the air unhappily. He moves his huge head from side to side. Six feet high that head towers with its immense frill of bone. Down close to the ground is his parrot-beak nose. Its small horn points straight ahead. Between his eyes are the other two horns which make him "Three-Horn-Face." They reach out three feet or more ahead, and their sharp points slice the air as Three-Horn moves his head.

From his nose to the end of his thick tail, Triceratops stretches between twenty and thirty feet long. His skull alone is five feet long, with its towering frill.

Three-Horn is not speedy, but his thick legs are full of power. He can lunge straight ahead like a bulldozer, and woe to anyone who gets in the path of those on-coming horns!

Who would dare face Triceratops? There is one hungry giant who will. This is meat-eating, roaring, snorting, tearing, slashing Tyrannosaurus, the Tyrant Lizard. Sometimes men add Rex or King to his name. For surely he must have been the ruler of his world. He was huge. He was powerful. He had to kill to live, and there were few creatures of his time he could not kill.

Here comes Tyrannosaurus now. He towers twenty feet tall as he pounds along on his clawed hind feet. His tail swishes heavily over the ground behind him. From head to tail he measures forty feet maybe more than the length of your house!

Up at the height of a second-storey window his great head sways. His head alone is longer than you are tall. Wide nostrils sniff for the smell of fresh meat. A huge mouth yawns like a dreadful red door. It is rimmed with teeth, each tooth six inches long and as sharp as a sword.

The thick skin hangs down from the Tyrant Lizard's neck in loose, empty folds. He has not had a good big meal for some time. But now he spies Triceratops. Those thick, meaty shanks would fill the Tyrant's huge stomach nicely!

Slowly, heavily he begins to circle around Three-Horn. He does not want to attack from the front because of those horns. He wants a bite at Three-Horn's unprotected side instead.

The Tyrant moves closer. Three-Horn stands firm. His horns are lowered for action, but unfortunately for him his mind does not work fast. While Three-Horn just stands there, Tyrant Lizard circles a clump of bushes—and lunges!

A heavy-clawed hind foot rips Three-Horn's flank. The Tyrant's sword-sharp teeth reach for Three-Horn's windpipe.

But Three-Horn has not lost the fight. Not yet! He has special weapons for defence. His skull is balanced on a handy ball-and-socket joint below his bony frill, and attached to the bottom of that bony frill are huge and powerful neck muscles. His leg muscles are very powerful too. Putting all these muscles and joints to work, Three-Horn manages to turn under the Tyrant's attack. He lunges sideways, and he catches the Tyrant in the ribs with those two sharp horns of his! There is a thunder-sharp crack of snapping bones! With a roar of rage and pain, the Tyrant rears back. His small fore-claws flail at Three-Horn, but he does not want to risk another jab from those horns.

Three-Horn just stands there. He may not be clever, but he can look after himself.

With another roar, Tyrant Lizard shuffles away to rest and lick his wounds. He is really tired. Like all cold-blooded animals, he tires quickly, and this has been a hard day for him.

TYRANNOSAURUS

PACHYCEPHALOSAURUS

NEXT DAY, down along the sunny shore, Tyrant Lizard finds the hunting better. He can walk fairly fast on his two legs on dry land. But he does not like to get too close to the water. For he weighs eight tons or more. His clawed feet sink deep in soft mud or sand. He may get stuck completely. At best he is slowed down.

Sometimes the duck-billed dinosaurs along the shore come back onto dry ground. That is what Tyrant Lizard is hoping for. Duck-bills are big enough to make a good meal, and they do not have sharp horns and spikes.

Or do they? There is Lambeosaurus now. And on his head he wears a crest shaped like a double-

255 million years ago 256 257 258 259 260 26

DIPLOVERTEBRON

bladed hatchet. This crest has hollow bones to hold air.

Lambeosaurus can hide under water for some time, though Tyrant Lizard does not know that. He does seem to know that the crest will not harm him.

Hungrily the Tyrant watches Lambeosaurus. Soon the duck-bill walks away over the sand on

Here comes Pachycephalosaurus, Thick-Headed Lizard. He belongs to a group of rather small dinosaurs related to the duck-bills.

Pachycephalosaurus has a small brain. But he has good protection for it. His brain is protected by a dome of solid skull bone nine inches thick! The outside of his head is decorated with extra bumps and points of bone.

LAMBEOSAURUS

his broad, webbed feet. Then out into the water he goes, and he drops to all four feet for a lunch of water plants.

Tyrannosaurus swishes his tail angrily. He cannot follow Lambeosaurus there, and he is getting impatient, and hungrier still. But he does not have much longer to wait.

Tyrant Lizard does not care about that thick skull. He does not mind the bony bumps on Thick Head's face. They cannot hurt him. He is interested in Thick Head's plumpness. He is interested in food. So he lunges with tooth and claw!

Down goes Pachycephalosaurus, and Tyrant Lizard has a good meal at last.

RIDING THE SWELLS of this broad inland sea is a bird. It seems very large to us. For it is more than four feet long. It is Hesperornis or Western Bird. Off in the distance float more of the same kind. They look much like the diving birds which swim on lakes of today.

Now and then we see one dive for a fish. But as long as we may watch, we shall never see one fly. For these are birds which have lost their power of flight. Through ages of living on the sea, their wings have disappeared.

So Hesperornis cannot fly. It cannot even walk or stand. For its webbed paddle feet on short legs are set at the back of its body. It could not keep its balance if it tried to stand on those legs.

On water, though, Hesperornis is completely at home. It swims very well. The feet are just right for that, and its sharp teeth can snatch plenty of fishes for food.

There are plenty of fishes in these waters. Fishes have lived on since before the days of reptiles and amphibians. They were the first creatures to have

skeletons made of bone, and most of the families we know today—the herring, the swordfish, the sturgeon and pike, the sharks (whose skeletons are made of cartilage instead of bone) and others—were already swimming ancient seas as long ago as Cretaceous times.

But there are also "reptiles" of the seas. These are reptiles which, like the bird Hesperornis, have lost their ability to live on land. They live in the sea instead.

Ichthyosaurus, the Fish Lizard, has been swimming the oceans of the world since back in Triassic times. (We saw a member of his family in the world of 150 million years ago.) But Ichthyosaurus is not the only one.

Near by, Elasmosaurus or Thin-Plate Lizard rows himself peacefully along. His long, paddle-shaped limbs serve as oars. They move with slow, smooth strokes. For Elasmosaurus is not in a hurry.

There is no need for speed. His flat, broad body is not built for it. His head moves fast enough. On his long, thin neck his head can dart swiftly this way and that. He can reach out twenty feet in any direction. He can surprise a lot of fish!

ELASMOSAURUS

7 278 279 280 281 282 283 284

ICHTHYOSTEGA

Elasmosaurus is forty feet long. Much of that length is in his snake-like neck. In fact, one early English scientist described him as "a snake drawn through the body of a turtle." His body is really not much different in size from that of twelve-foot Archelon, the Ruler Turtle of the seas.

At the end of his snaky neck, Elasmosaurus has jaws full of long, sharp-pointed teeth. They can snap swiftly shut on a swimming fish.

Also he has such strong leg muscles that he can paddle backward as well as ahead. So Elasmosaurus does not go hungry, even though he may not be swift.

Elasmosaurus is just one member of the Plesiosaur, or Near-Lizard, family. Another is Trinacromerum. He has a shorter neck and a larger jaw. He is in the picture below along with Archelon.

His legs have turned to flippers too. But the bones in them are still strong enough so that Trinacromerum, like many other members of his family, can go ashore if he wishes, and he can pull himself about there as seals do on rocky beaches today.

See the wild-looking giant with Elasmosaurus. This is Tylosaurus, a twenty-footer of the Mosasaur family. Tylosaurus, as you can see, is not as sleek and fish-like as Ichthyosaurus. Like Ichthyosaurus, it swishes along through the water by side-wise motions of its body and tail. It swims like a fish, and it uses its paddle-like limbs just to keep its balance in the water. What gives it a wild and dangerous look is its huge, tooth-filled jaws.

Mosasaurs are called sea lizards, and they really are lizards which went back to the sea to live. They get along so well in the sea that they have grown to be giant sea-serpents. They are the size of some of our whales of today.

ARCHELON **TRINACROMERUM**

Reptiles of Today

END OF AN ERA

Close of the Cretaceous Period, End of the Age of Reptiles

The world is changing. Dry plains are rising up where, not long ago, quiet shallow seas lapped softly at their shores. Hardwood forests tower in place of tender ferns and palms.

This new world is no place for dinosaurs. As the swamps shrink, their food supply dwindles. And they have not the brains to work out how to find new foods. Among the close-growing trees of the new forests, they cannot move easily. So the last of the giants wander sadly. At last they sink down, many of them weakened by disease or hunger.

The small, furry mammals are growing in size and numbers. They are beginning to spread over the world. Mammals like the shelter of the new forests. The first of their kind have been hiding in tree branches for many millions of years. This is a good world for them.

The mammals have bigger brains, too, than the dinosaurs. They can work out how to get food, and, once in a while, the food they find themselves may be dinosaur eggs. Or they may even feast on a fallen giant himself.

So the mammals prosper. Their great day is dawning. (The day of the mammals is still going on. We are living in it. We are mammals too.)

Meanwhile the dinosaurs die off, often leaving no eggs or young behind them. One by one, whole families vanish. The horned beasts of the high country are the last to go. But as the period of time we call the Cretaceous slips slowly into the past, every dinosaur has vanished from the earth.

No longer does the ground shake under the heavy tramp of Tyrannosaurus Rex. No more do broad-winged flying lizards flap across the skies. They have vanished too. Even the great lizards in the seas have vanished. No more do the Mosasaurs and Plesiosaurs and Ichthyosaurs snap at passing fish. They seemed perfectly suited to their life. It seemed that nothing could stop them. But, with their great cousins the dinosaurs, the swimming reptiles vanished mysteriously from the world.

There are a few reptiles which live on. Crocodiles and alligators still slither along in tropical streams. Lizards, built a bit like miniature dinosaurs, still drowse on rocks in the sun. Tortoises and turtles still go their quiet way, much as they did almost 200 million years ago.

Birds, which developed from reptiles, still swoop and soar across our skies, but not a dinosaur do we see. No man has ever seen a living dinosaur. For, millions of years before the first man lived, the day of the dinosaurs was done.

CERATOPSIANS
(horned dinosaurs)
ORNITHOPODS
(duck-billed dinosaurs)
THEROPODS
(carnivorous dinosaurs)
ANKYLOSAURS
(armored dinosaurs)
ORNITHOPODS
(duck-billed dinosaurs)
SAUROPODS
(giant dinosaurs)
THEROPODS
(carnivorous dinosaurs)